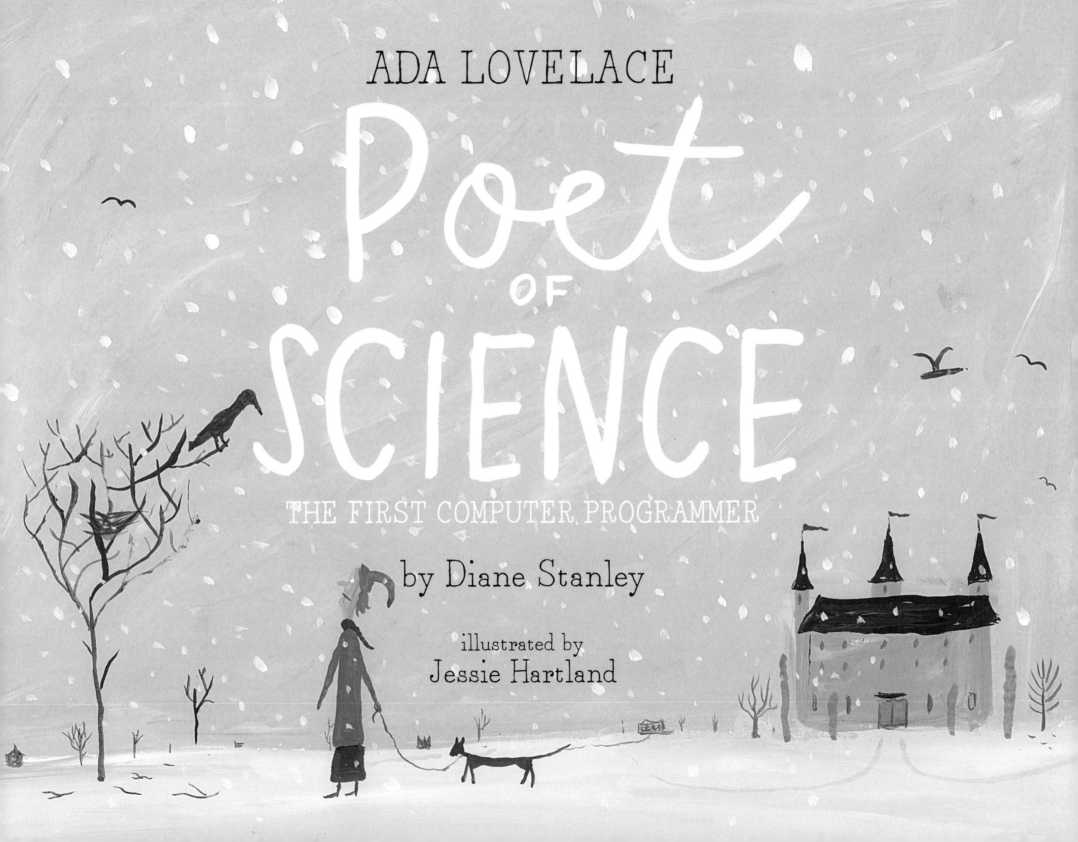

ADA LOVELACE

Poet OF SCIENCE

THE FIRST COMPUTER PROGRAMMER

by Diane Stanley

illustrated by
Jessie Hartland

Long, long ago, on a cold winter day, a lonely little girl walked from room to room in a big, old, dark country house.

Her name was Ada Byron
and she was looking for
something to do.

Lord Byron

Ada was good at imagining things. She imagined it would be fun to fly. Then she went about it in a scientific way. First she studied the flight and the anatomy of birds.

She decided her wings would be like theirs, only larger, in proportion to her size. She would build the frames out of sturdy wire so her wings would be strong, then cover the frames with oil-rubbed silk so they would also be light. Finally, she designed a harness to attach the wings to her back.

She thought it would be fun to fly from house to house delivering the mail.

She'd need to bring a bag for carrying the letters, a map, and a compass for navigation.

She decided to write a book about her flying project, illustrated with pictures and diagrams.

She would call it *Flyology*.

And when she had finished that, Ada had a plan to build a steam-powered flying horse.

Her mother, Lady Byron, was away at the time,
so Ada sent regular updates on the flying project.
She signed the letters, "Your affectionate young
Turkey" or "Your affectionate Carrier Pigeon."

She had never been so happy.

But Lady Byron was worried.

London
1828

Dear
Mammy,

Hello

Lady Byron

your affectionate
carrier pigeon,

Ada seemed overexcited. Worse, she showed
dangerous signs of too much imagination.

In other words, she was acting like her father.

Ada's parents were as different as chalk and cheese. Her father, the famous poet Lord Byron, was a worldwide celebrity, the rock star of his time.

LORD BYRON

LADY BYRON

Her mother, Lady Byron, was interested in math and science.

She was rational, respectable, and strict. The marriage only lasted a year.

Ada never knew her father. He left England soon after she was born and died in faraway Greece when she was eight. She wasn't even sure what he looked like. His portrait had been covered with a cloth. Being Lord Byron's daughter shaped Ada's childhood in important ways.

BIRDS

Lord Byron

Ada's mother wanted her to be calm and rational, not emotional and creative like her father. She hoped the study of math and science would suppress her daughter's imagination. So Ada was given a world-class scientific education.

Physics
CHEMISTRY
BIOLOGY
mechanical
Engineering
ASTRONOMY

GEOMETRY

GEOMETRY

Math

Her imagination was not harmed in the least.

Ada loved machines. She lived during the Industrial Revolution, when things that were once made by hand—from ribbons and spoons to paper and glass—were being mass-produced in factories.

When Lady Bryon suggested a trip to see the new factories, Ada was thrilled to go.

Everything they saw was interesting. But by far the best was the mechanical loom designed by a Frenchman, Joseph Marie Jacquard. It could automatically weave cloth in any design you could imagine, from a simple plaid, to fancy brocade, to actual pictures of people, trees, and animals.

LOOMS

SHROPSHIRE TEXTILES

TEXTILE MILLS

But how did the loom know which pattern to weave? That was the amazing part. The design was translated into a pattern of holes punched into heavy paper cards. Long chains of these cards were fed into the loom, giving it instructions. To change the design, you only had to change the cards. Ada was amazed. It was a brilliant idea—and not just for weaving cloth.

Why not use punched cards to direct other machines for other purposes?

Ada was onto something.
Soon she would see how right she was.

At seventeen, Ada's quiet childhood came to an end.

Her mother took her to London for the summer social season, a round of teas, dinners, and dances.

Ada was dazzled by the gilded ballrooms and the beautiful ladies in their gleaming satin gowns.

Everyone wanted to meet Ada because she was Lord Byron's daughter.

Hatters Ltd.

HYDE PARK

But Ada didn't know what to say to them.
She didn't care about fashion, fox hunting, or court gossip.

Then she went to one of the weekly gatherings at the home of Charles Babbage, the great mathematician and inventor.

All the interesting people went to his parties, from the writer Charles Dickens to the scientist Charles Darwin. As Ada moved through the crowd, from one amazing conversation to another, she grew almost dizzy with excitement.

They talked about important things: astronomy and politics, literature and art, and the latest engineering marvels. *These* were her kind of people.

A few days later, Ada went to see a working portion of Babbage's new invention: a calculating machine called the Difference Engine.

Difference Engine

It could solve arithmetic problems at the turn of a crank.

TEA

People called it a thinking machine, but Ada knew better. The intelligence was not in the machine itself, but in the genius of its designer.

Ada felt an instant connection with Charles Babbage. She even dreamed of one day helping with his important work.

And so began one of the most remarkable friendships in the history of science.

But Lady Byron had other plans for her daughter. Ada didn't need a profession. What she needed was a husband. So at nineteen Ada married a wealthy aristocrat, William, Lord King. When he became the Earl of Lovelace, Ada Byron King changed her name once again. She would go down in history as Ada Lovelace.

By the time she was twenty-four, Ada had two children running wild in the nursery and one still crying in his cradle.

But she hadn't lost sight of her dream, just postponed it.

Now at last her moment had come.

Babbage was working on a revolutionary new machine called the Analytical Engine.

It would be powered by steam (there was no electricity in those days) and it could do much more than just add and subtract.

The Analytical Engine could run any kind of mathematical calculation, then store the results for later use. Best of all, he had borrowed Jacquard's idea of using punched cards to direct his Engine, so it could easily change from one operation to another.

In short, Charles Babbage had invented the first fully programmable all-purpose digital computer.

But there was a problem. So far his Engine was just a plan on paper. It would cost a fortune to build. To raise that kind of money, Babbage needed publicity.

This was Ada's chance to help. An article had been written about the Analytical Engine, but it was in French. Ada translated it into English so it could be published in Britain.

Then Babbage asked her to add some footnotes at the end, explaining what an all-purpose computing machine could do.

She was perfect for the job. She understood how the engine worked. She was a good writer. And she had the vision to see, better even than Babbage himself, how much more a computer could do besides just processing numbers.

It could work with any kind of symbol, from words to musical notes.

Ada imagined the Analytical Engine writing text, composing music, reproducing images— even playing games like checkers or chess.

Numbers of Bernoulli

$$-\frac{1}{2} \cdot \frac{2n-1}{2n+1} + B_1\left(\frac{2n}{2}\right) +$$

$$+B_3\left(\frac{2n \cdot (2n-1) \cdot (2n-2)}{2 \cdot 3 \cdot 4}\right)$$

$$+B_5\left(\frac{2n \cdot (2n-1) \dots (2n-4)}{2 \cdot 3 \cdot 4 \cdot 5 \cdot 6}\right) \Bigg\} \; 8.$$

$$+ \dots B_{2n-1}$$

newtonian physics
PHYSICS

Bernoulli

But before the machine could do any of those things, the symbols and rules of operation had to be changed into digital form.

Today we call that programming.

Ada needed to explain to her readers exactly how that could be done.

1

As an example to work with, she and Babbage chose an extremely complicated series of calculations called the numbers of Bernoulli. And then Ada showed, step-by-tiny-step, how they could be coded for the machine.

2

3

7

8

9

Finally, after nine months of meticulous work,

Sketch of the Analytical Engine Invented by Charles Babbage was published.

4

6

10

Ada's "Notes by the Translator" were almost three times as long as the original article—and far more important. Yet she wasn't credited by name, only the initials A.A.L.

11

by A.A.L.

She was afraid her work wouldn't be taken seriously if people knew it was written by a woman.

12

Ada didn't care. The girl who had once dreamed of flying, who longed to do something important with her mind, had soared at last. She had looked into the future and imagined a computer age that wouldn't arrive for another hundred years.

And in demonstrating how to code the numbers of Bernoulli, Ada Lovelace had written the first computer program ever published.

AUTHOR'S NOTE

Ada did not live to write another scientific paper. Sadly, she died of cancer at the age of thirty-six, the same age as her famous father. Babbage's Analytical Engine was never built, and in his later years he was dismissed as a failure. Though their partnership marked the beginning of the computer age, there is no direct link between their work and the development of the modern computer. Babbage's groundbreaking invention and Ada's visionary writings were forgotten.

Years later, Ada's translation and *Notes* resurfaced. We know that Alan Turing, the computer pioneer who helped break the Nazi Enigma Code, had read them. He was especially interested in her assertion that computers were incapable of original thought. He called this "Lady Lovelace's objection." Howard Aiken, who helped design the Harvard Mark I for IBM, read them too. "If Babbage had lived seventy-five years later," he said, "I would have been out of a job."

In 1991, a full replica of the Difference Engine #2 was successfully built by a team from London's Science Museum (www.sciencemuseum.org.uk). It worked perfectly. In 2011 the same team launched a second, far more ambitious effort, this time to build the enormous and vastly more complex Analytical Engine. They expect the job to take ten years. Stay tuned!

CONTROVERSY

About twenty-five years ago, several scholars raised the question of whether Ada really wrote the *Notes* or Babbage did it for her. Certainly they worked together. But no one who has read the many letters they exchanged or the pertinent sections of Babbage's biography can doubt that Ada was the true author. All agree that Babbage worked out the complicated series of numbers of Bernoulli, a laborious job, to save Ada the trouble when she was sick, and that Ada found an error he'd made and corrected it. But it was Ada who coded those numbers for the Analytical Engine. Babbage himself said that she did the "algebraic working out of the different problems." And it's obvious from the letters that she added the table and diagram that showed exactly how the instructions would be broken down into specific steps. On the basis of this evidence, the vast majority of scholars consider Ada's algorithm to be the first computer program.

Portrait by Alfred Chalon, 1838. Public Domain.

IMPORTANT DATES

1804 – Joseph Marie Jacquard invents an automated loom controlled by punched cards

1815 – (January 2) George Gordon Byron, 6th Baron Byron (commonly known as Lord Byron) marries Anne Isabella (Annabella) Milbanke. (December 10) Augusta Ada Byron is born in London

1816 – (January 16) Lord and Lady Byron separate (April 25) Lord Byron leaves England

1824 – (April 19) Lord Byron dies in Greece at the age of 36

1828 – Ada attempts to invent a flying machine

1833 – Ada meets Charles Babbage and sees his Difference Engine

1834 – Babbage begins work on the Analytical Engine

1835 – (July 8) Ada marries William King (three children are born to the marriage: Byron, 1836; Annabella, 1837; and Ralph Gordon, 1839)

1840 – Babbage gives a speech about the Analytical Engine in Turin, Italy; an article about it by Luigi Menabrea appears in a Swiss scientific journal

1842 – Ada hires a tutor and returns to the study of mathematics

1843 – Ada's translation and *Notes* are published

1852 – (November 27) Ada dies of cancer. She is buried beside her father in a small church near the Byron ancestral home

1871 – (October 18) Charles Babbage dies

1931 – MIT professor Vannevar Bush builds the differential analyzer, the first modern analog computer

1936 – Alan Turing develops the "Turing Machine"

1944 – The Harvard Mark I is built by IBM

1946 – ENIAC (Electronic Numerical Integrator and Computer), the first electronic digital computer, is built by the US Army

1977 – 1983 – The US Department of Defense develops a software language designed to unite other computer languages and names it "Ada" in honor of Ada Lovelace

2009 – Annual International Ada Lovelace Day is declared in London to raise awareness of women in STEM (Science, Technology, Engineering, and Math) fields

2012 – (December 10) Ada Lovelace is honored with a Google Doodle on her 197th birthday (www.theguardian.com/technology/2012/dec/10/ada-lovelace-honoured-google-doodle)

SELECTED BIBLIOGRAPHY

Collier, Bruce and MacLachlan, James. *Charles Babbage and the Engines of Perfection.* New York/Oxford: Oxford University Press, 1998.

Essinger, James. *Ada's Algorithm: How Lord Byron's Daughter Ada Lovelace Launched the Digital Age.* Brooklyn/London: Melville House, 2014.

Isaacson, Walter. *The Innovators: How a Group of Hackers, Geniuses, and Geeks Created the Digital Revolution.* New York: Simon and Schuster, 2014.

Swade, Doron. *The Difference Engine: Charles Babbage and the Quest to Build the First Computer.* New York: Penguin Books, 2001.

Toole, Betty Alexandra. *Ada, the Enchantress of Numbers: Poetical Science.* Sausalito, California: Critical Connection, 1992.

Toole, Betty Alexandra. *Ada, the Enchantress of Numbers: A Selection from the Letters of Lord Byron's Daughter and Her Description of the First Computer.* Mill Valley, California: Strawberry Press, 1992.

Woolley, Benjamin. *The Bride of Science: Romance, Reason, and Byron's Daughter.* New York: McGraw-Hill, 1999.

GLOSSARY

Anatomy—the physical form of an animal or plant. For example, the anatomy of a bird would include the size, shape, and design of every part of its body, from its bones, muscles, and organs to its feathers, beak, and claws.

Automatic—an action, usually performed by a machine, which is done without any outside control, such as automatic door-openers.

Calculate—to find an answer to a problem mathematically, such as adding, subtracting, multiplying, or dividing.

Code—another word for programming.

Digital computer—a computer in which all data, including words, sounds, or images, is entered in the form of numbers, usually combinations of zeroes and ones.

Mechanical—something done by a machine or in an automatic, machine-like way.

Numbers of Bernoulli—an extremely complicated sequence of numbers named after the Swiss mathematician Jakob Bernoulli and connected to number theory.

Operation—an action done by a computer, such as adding numbers, processing words, or making digital images.

Program/Programmer/Programmable—all modern computers are "programmable." This means they do more than one thing. Depending on which task you want a computer to perform—write words, make pictures, do math calculations—a programmer first has to translate those instructions into a digital language, called a "program" or "algorithm."

Rational—a person or idea that is logical and sensible; thoughts and judgments based on reason and science.

For Clementine —D. S.
This one's for Peter Steele, my other red-haired nephew
and a dreamer—like Ada Lovelace—J. H.

The publisher gratefully acknowledges Dr. Betty A. Toole for reviewing this book for accuracy.

SIMON & SCHUSTER BOOKS FOR YOUNG READERS
An imprint of Simon & Schuster Children's Publishing Division
1230 Avenue of the Americas, New York, New York 10020

For information about special discounts for bulk purchases, please contact Simon & Schuster Special Sales at 1-866-506-1949 or business@simonandschuster.com.
The Simon & Schuster Speakers Bureau can bring authors to your live event. For more information or to book an event, contact the Simon & Schuster Speakers Bureau at 1-866-248-3049 or visit our website at www.simonspeakers.com.
Book design by Greg Stadnyk
The text for this book was set in Slimtype.
The illustrations for this book was rendered in gouache.
Manufactured in China
0716 SCP
First Edition
2 4 6 8 10 9 7 5 3 1
Library of Congress Cataloging-in-Publication Data
Stanley, Diane, author.
Ada Lovelace, poet of science: the first computer programmer / Diane Stanley ; illustrated by Jessie Hartland.—1st edition.
pages cm
"A Paula Wiseman Book."
Summary: "A fascinating look at Ada Lovelace, the pioneering computer programmer and daughter of the poet Lord Byron."—Provided by publisher.
Audience: Ages 4–8
Audience: Grades K to 3
ISBN 978-1-4814-5249-6 (hardcover)—ISBN 978-1-4814-5250-2 (eBook) 1. Lovelace, Ada King, Countess of, 1815–1852—Juvenile literature.
2. Babbage, Charles, 1791–1871—Juvenile literature. 3. Women mathematicians—Great Britain—Biography—Juvenile literature. 4. Women computer programmers—Great Britain—Biography—Juvenile literature. 5. Mathematicians—Great Britain—Biography—Juvenile literature. 6. Computers—History—19th century—Juvenile literature.
I. Hartland, Jessie, illustrator. II. Title.
QA29.L72S73 2016
510.92—dc23 [B]
2015010872